GO FACTS SEASONS

Summer

A & C BLACK • LONDON

Summer

© Blake Publishing 2003
Additional material © A & C Black Publishers Ltd 2005

First published 2003 in Australia by Blake Education Pty Ltd

This edition published 2005 in the United Kingdom by
A & C Black Publishers Ltd, 37 Soho Square, London W1D 3QZ
www.acblack.com

ISBN-10: 0-7136-7268-4
ISBN-13: 978-0-7136-7268-8

A CIP record for this book is available from the British Library.

Written by Katy Pike
Design and layout by The Modern Art Production Group
Photos by John Foxx, Photodisc, Corel, Brand X, Corbis, Digital Stock,
Rubberball, Image Source, Superstock, Eyewire and Artville.

UK series consultant: Julie Garnett

Printed in China by WKT Company Ltd.

A & C Black uses paper produced with elemental chlorine-free pulp,
harvested from managed sustainable forests.

Contents

 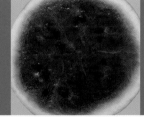

Signs of Summer

As spring turns to summer, what changes can you see and feel?

Summer days are long. Plants grow quickly and flower. Trees are covered in green leaves.

Summer is a good time to play outside or go swimming. People wear light clothes and often take holidays.

Beaches are popular in summer.

GO FACT!

LONGEST!
The longest day of the year is called the summer solstice, on June 21st or 22nd.

Red poppies flower in the summer.

5

Plants in Summer

Plants grow quickly in summer.

Many plants flower in summer. Flowers make seeds. Some flowers, like apple blossoms, become fruit. Fruits grow and **ripen** in the summer.

In summer, trees are covered in green leaves. The leaves make food for the tree. The **trunk** grows thicker.

Summer oak leaves

6

This tree's trunk will grow thicker during the summer.

This cut tree trunk shows one ring for each year of growth.

Cherries are a summer fruit.

Gardening is fun in summer. Everything grows so quickly.

Maize and sunflowers grow taller each day. Tomatoes, cucumbers and beans ripen. Then they are ready to pick and eat.

Grass grows quickly too. Mowing the **lawn** is a summer chore for some people.

Sunflower

TALLEST!
The tallest sunflower grew to more than 25 feet tall. That's as tall as a 2-storey building.

Summer gardens grow quickly if they get enough water.

Summer Food

We eat more fresh food in summer.

Salads are made from fresh summer vegetables. Families enjoy the outdoors by having picnics and barbecues.

Many fruits, such as berries, melons and peaches, are ripe in the summer. Fruit salad is good for you and it tastes good too.

Vegetable salad

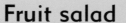

Fruit salad

GO FACT!

HOTTEST!
The hottest world record temperature was in the Sahara Desert: 58°C in 1922.

What fresh fruits and vegetables are on the picnic table?

11

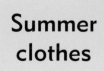

On hot summer days people try to keep cool.

People wear light clothes in summer. We wear sandals, shorts and T-shirts.

Swimming is another way people keep cool. Crowds gather at pools and beaches in the summer.

The long school break is in the summer. Many families take holidays.

Summer clothes

You can see the underwater world when snorkelling.

Sunscreen protects people's skin.

Hot summers sometimes bring forest fires.

13

There is plenty of food for animals to eat in summer.

The animals that were born in the spring are growing. Baby birds grow adult feathers. Foxes and badgers come out of their dens to look for food.

Butterfly

In summer, **insects** are everywhere. Bees, butterflies and other kinds of bugs feed on plants.

From tiny insects to large **mammals**, animals are busy eating their way through the summer.

14

Young toads climb out of the water in June or July.

Midges spend their short lives eating and laying eggs.

Squirrels build a nest, called a drey, in summer.

Glossary

insect	a small animal with three main body parts and six legs
lawn	grass that is kept mowed
mammal	an animal that feeds its babies with milk
ripen	become ready to eat
summer	the warmest part of the year
trunk	the central woody part of a tree

Index